How CIOs Can Solve the Security Puzzle

Tips And Techniques For CIOs To Use In Order To Secure Both Their IT Department And Their Company

"Practical, proven techniques that will show you how to help your IT department to make the department and the company more secure"

Dr. Jim Anderson

Published by:
Blue Elephant Consulting
Tampa, Florida

Printed in the United States of America

Library of Congress Control Number: 2014951295

ISBN-13: 978-1502369574
ISBN-10: 1502369575

Warning – Disclaimer

The purpose of this book is to educate and entertain. This book does not promise or guarantee that anyone following the ideas, tips, suggestions, techniques or strategies will be successful. The author, publisher and distributor(s) shall have neither liability nor responsibility to anyone with respect to any loss or damage caused, or alleged to be caused, directly or indirectly by the information contained in this book.

Recent Books By The Author

Product Management

- How Product Managers Can Grow Their Career: How Product Managers Can Find And Succeed In The Right Job

- Product Management Secrets: Techniques For Product Managers To Boost Product Sales And Increase Customer Satisfaction

Public Speaking

- How To Become A Better Speaker By Changing How You Speak: Change techniques that will transform a speech into a memorable event

- How To Give A Great Presentation: Presentation techniques that will transform a speech into a memorable event

CIO Skills

- What CIOs Need To Know About Working With Partners: Techniques For CIOs To Use In Order To Be Able To Successfully Work With Partners

- How CIOs Can Make Innovation Happen: Tips And Techniques For CIOs To Use In Order To Make Innovation Happen In Their IT Department

IT Manager Skills

- How IT Managers Can Make Innovation Happen: Tips And Techniques For IT Managers To Use In Order To Make Innovation Happen In Their Teams

- Secrets Of Effective Leadership For IT Managers: Tips And Techniques That IT Managers Can Use In Order To Develop Leadership Skills

Negotiating

- Learn How To Signal In Your Next Negotiation: How To Develop The Skill Of Effective Signaling In A Negotiation In Order To Get The Best Possible Outcome

- Learn The Skill Of Exploring In A Negotiation: How To Develop The Skill Of Exploring What Is Possible In A Negotiation In Order To Reach The Best Possible Deal

Miscellaneous

- The Internet-Enabled Successful School District Superintendent: How To Use The Internet To Boost Parental Involvement In Your Schools

- Power Distribution Unit (PDU) Secrets: What Everyone Who Works In A Data Center Needs To Know!

Note: See a complete list of books by Dr. Jim Anderson at the back of this book.

4

Acknowledgements

Any book like this one is the result of years of real-world work experience. In my over 25 years of working for 7 different firms, I have met countless fantastic people and I've been mentored by some truly exceptional ones. Although I've probably forgotten some of the people who made me the person that I am today, here is my attempt to finally give them the recognition that they so truly deserve:

- Thomas P. Anderson
- Art Puett
- Bobbi Marshall
- Bob Boggs

Dr. Jim Anderson

This book is dedicated to my family: Lori, Maddie, Nick, and Ben. None of this would have been possible without their constant love and support.

Thanks for always believing in me and providing me with the strength to always be willing to go out there and be my best for you.

Blue Elephant Consulting
Speaking.   Negotiating.   Managing.   Marketing.

Table Of Contents

Securing The IT Department And The Company Is Part Of Being The CIO

As though staying on top of changing technology trends wasn't enough, today's CIOs also find themselves being held responsible for securing the IT department as well as the rest of the company. This is a job that few of us have ever been trained to do; however, the stakes have never been higher.

Your company's senior management knows even less about IT security than you do. However, they view you as being the person who can keep them safe. If you can accomplish this task, then you will have secured your relationship with the CEO and CFO, if not then they may be looking for a new CIO.

In order to successful secure your department and your company, you are going to have to start at the network's endpoints and work your way in. This will involve creating security policies that everyone can live with and performing routine vulnerability management studies.

The key to any successful securing of a corporate network is to make sure that only the right people and applications are allowed to be there. This means that you'll need to implement an effective identify management program. You'll have to do the same thing for the applications that run on the company's network by creating a whitelisting solution that ensures that you are only executing the code that should be run.

At times dealing with the wide variety of IT security threats that your company will be facing will seem to be overwhelming. However, by taking the time to listen to what reformed hackers have to tell us, you'll be able to prioritize the threats and focus your time and energy where they'll do the most good.

This book has been written in order to provide you with a great starting point for ensuring that you've done everything that you can to protect your company. We'll show you what you need to take care of and how the bad guys are going to try to break into your networks. Follow the suggestions in this book and you'll have successfully secured your company's IT resources.

For more information on what it takes to be a great CIO, check out my blog, The Accidental Successful CIO, at:

www.TheAccidentalSuccessfulCIO.com

Good luck!

-     Dr. Jim Anderson

About The Author

I must confess that I never set out to be a CIO. When I went to school, I studied Computer Science and thought that I'd get a nice job programming and that would be that. Well, at least part of that plan worked out!

My first job was working for Boeing on their F/A-18 fighter jet program. I spent my days programming fighter jet software in assembly language and I loved it. The U.S. government decided to save some money and went looking for other countries to sell this plane to. This put me into an unfamiliar role: I started to meet with foreign military officials and I ended up having to manage groups of engineers who were working on international projects.

Time moved on and so did I. I found myself working for Siemens, the big German telecommunications company. They were making phone switches and selling them to the seven U.S. phone companies. The problem was that the switches were too complicated. Customers couldn't tell the difference between one complicated phone switch from another complicated phone switch. Once again I found myself working with the sales and marketing teams to find ways to make the great technology that the engineers had developed understandable to both internal and external customers.

I've spent over 25 years working as an senior IT professional for both big companies and startups. This has given me an opportunity to learn what it takes to manage and IT department in ways that allow it to maximize its output while becoming a valuable part of the overall company.

I now live in Tampa Florida where I spend my time managing my consulting business, Blue Elephant Consulting, teaching college courses at the University of South Florida, and traveling to work with companies like yours to share the knowledge that I have about how to create and manage successful IT departments.

I'm always available to answer questions and I can be reached at:

Dr. Jim Anderson
Blue Elephant Consulting
Email: jim@BlueElephantConsulting.com
Facebook: http://goo.gl/1TVoK
Web: **www.BlueElephantConsulting.com**

"Unforgettable communication skills that will set your ideas free..."

Create IT Departments That Are Productive And A Valuable Asset To The Rest Of The Company !

Dr. Jim Anderson is available to provide training and coaching on the topics that are the most important to people who have to manage IT departments: how can I build a productive IT department (and keep it together) while at the same time providing the rest of the company with the IT services that they need?

Dr. Anderson believes that in order to both learn and remember what he says, speakers need to laugh. Each one of his speeches is full of fun and humor so that what he says "sticks" with everyone.

Dr. Anderson's CIO SkillsTraining Includes:

1. How to identify and attract the right type of IT workers to your IT department.
2. How to build relationships with the company's senior management in order to get the support that you need?
3. How to stay on top of changing technology and security issues so that you never get surprised?

Dr. Jim Anderson works with over 100 customers per year. To invite Dr. Anderson to work with you, contact him at:

Phone: 813-418-6970 or
Email: jim@BlueElephantConsulting.com

Blue
Elephant
Consulting

Speaking. Negotiating. Managing. Marketing.

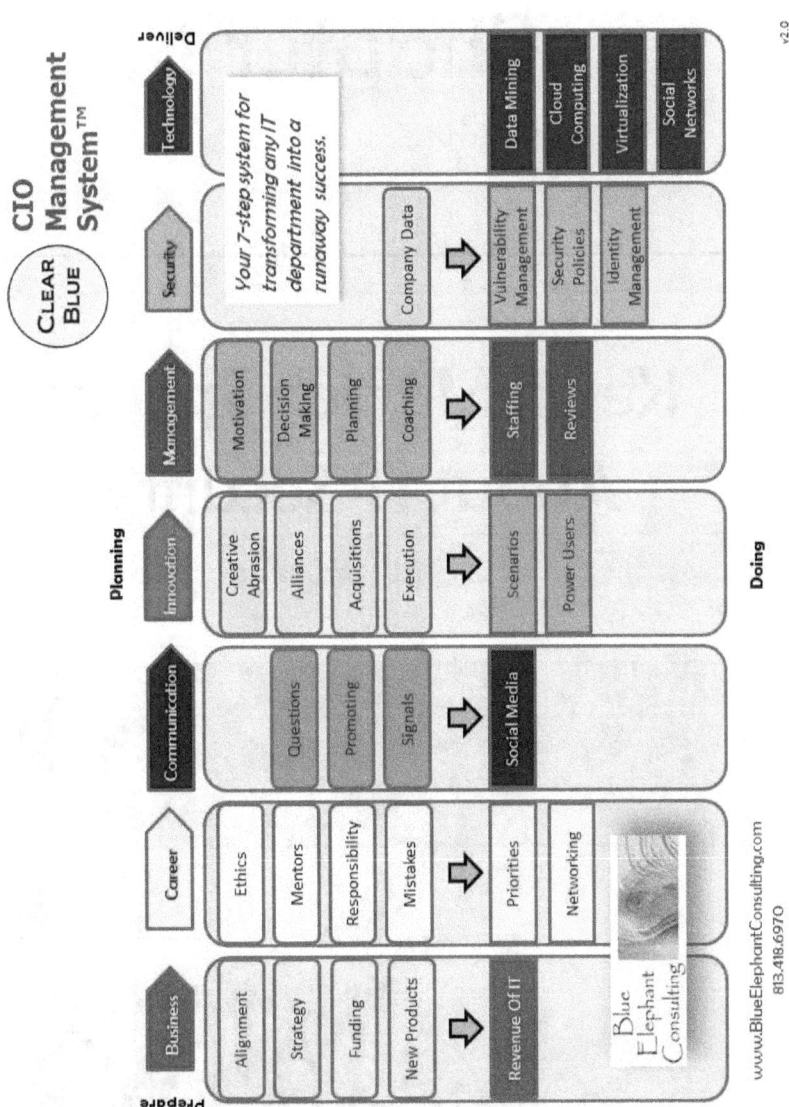

The **Clear Blue CIO Management System™** has been created to provide CIOs and senior IT managers with a clear roadmap for how to manage an IT department. This system shows CIOs what needs to be done and in what order to do it.

Chapter 1

Kevin Mitnick Speaks About IT Security

Chapter 1: Kevin Mitnick Speaks About IT Security

I had an opportunity to attend a very large IT health care show in Chicago awhile back and I was surprised to discover that Kevin Mitnick, the somewhat **infamous computer hacker**, was scheduled to give a speech.

Now even though I don't move in computer security circles that much, I know about Kevin Mitnick. I know about him because I read Tsutomu Shimomura's book *Takedown: The Pursuit and Capture of Kevin Mitnick, America's Most Wanted Computer Outlaw-By the Man Who Did It*. If you've never read the book, I can recommend it.

In a nutshell, Mitnick was a hacker who had evaded capture until he ticked off Shimomura who is a computer security pro. After he did that, Shimomura went after him with a vengeance and eventually **helped the authorities catch him and send him to jail**.

Now here in America, we all enjoy a good comeback story and that's basically what Kevin's been living. He has reinvented himself as a **computer security consultant** and by all accounts appears to be making a very nice living for himself.

Kevin Mitnick's Business Card Contains Lock Picking Tools – Talk About Unique!

Since getting out of prison, Kevin's been quite busy. He's an author and he's written two books: *The Art of Deception: Controlling the Human Element of Security* and *The Art of Intrusion: The Real Stories Behind the Exploits of Hackers, Intruders and Deceivers*.

Kevin is actually a pretty good speaker. The focus of the speech that he gave was to remind CIOs that no matter how much they have invested in firewalls, RSA tokens, and passwords that change every 90 days, it is **social engineering** that they need to fear the most.

Kevin's speech basically consisted of **stories** in which he would tell how he had broken into various computer systems using a variety of low-tech methods. These included making phone calls and asking for cell phone source code (thanks Motorola!) or simply doing dumpster diving to collect scraps of paper with usernames and passwords on them.

Kevin pointed out that one of the most valuable items that he had ever gotten his hands on was the **corporate directory** for GTE. Once he had this, he had everyone's phone number and knew who was the boss of who. With this info, he could place calls to get more and more information.

Kevin's stories and his continuing success on the right side of the law this time should serve as a reminder for all of us that at the end of the day, it's **the people who work in an IT department** that are your weakest link in security. If you fix this issue, then you'll be much closer to having a secure organization.

Chapter 2

Protecting Company Data Is How CIOs Can Make Friends with CFOs

Chapter 2: Protecting Company Data Is How CIOs Can Make Friends With CFOs

Data Security. There I said it. It sort of lays there like a big lump of coal and everyone in the company stands around looking at it wondering whose responsibility it is to **do something about it**. Nobody, including CIOs really wants to touch it for one very simple reason: it's a losing proposition.

How To Make Friends With Your CFO

Data security, despite being big, heavy, and ugly, always seems to end up in the CIOs lap. Since you really can't do anything to prevent this, it sure looks like this is a great opportunity to try to **turn a liability into an asset.**

Ericka Chickowski over at Baseline magazine has taken a look at this issue and come up with some interesting ways to help CIOs work more closely with CFOs. It all starts with **compliance**. Now compliance is just about as exciting as security; however, firms are willing to spend the big bucks on making sure that they are compliant because they know that there are potentially some **big financial penalties** if they don't.

It is the clever CIO that sits down with his / her CFO and explains that the company's data security program can be thought of as **an extension** of its compliance program. What this means is that you don't really need a separate program and your costs should be **much lower**. What CFO wouldn't be interested in hearing that?

Get Your Priorities In Order

One of the things that the CIO can learn from the compliance side of the house is that a critical first step is to make sure that you **prioritize the company data** that you are going to be protecting. All data is not created equal!

What's interesting here is that the importance of any single piece of information is based on **two things**: its value to the company and its role in keeping the company compliant. If your firm was a hospital, then clearly an electronic patient record would fall into the "top priority" bucket.

Act On Your Priorities – Not Necessarily Your Compliance

The level of protection that the IT department needs to surround a given piece of information with will depend on the result of this prioritization. I hope that you realize that this is just a fancy way of saying that there is some company data that you **DON'T** have to protect (or at least not very much).

Just about now you'd expect me to say that you should always go all out to protect ALL of your company data that is involved in a compliance program. But I'm not going to do that. Chickowski points out that **not all regulations are created equal**. In fact, some have fairly weak "teeth".

These are all things that the CIO and the CFO need to understand as they create a data protection plan / compliance program for the company. Spend those limited budget bucks to make sure that the important data is secure and then do what you can for the rest.

Final Thoughts

Within the company, the CFO **ALWAYS** wields more power than the CIO – money talks. Folding a company's data security program into its compliance program is a great way for a CIO to **work closely** with the CFO and should end up saving the firm money (always a good thing) and ensuring that it is both compliant and that its data is secure.

In addition to providing a CIO with a reason to talk to the CFO that doesn't involve begging for more money, an agreement about securing the company's data can allow CIOs to apply IT to enable the rest of the company to **grow quicker**, move faster, and do more.

Chapter 3

Vulnerability Management: The CIOs Other Job

Chapter 3: Vulnerability Management: The CIO's Other Job

The role of a CIO is to find ways to apply IT to enable the rest of the company to grow quicker, move faster, and do more. As part of this task a CIO needs to take steps to ensure that nothing happens that would prevent this from happening. This side of the job is not nearly as glamorous; however, it is at least as critical. What can a CIO do to ensure that **nothing bad happens** to a firm's IT systems?

The Job of Vulnerability Management

The first step in ensuring that a firm's IT systems continue to allow the company to move forward is to come to terms with the real world. This means that CIOs need to acknowledge that the world can be **an ugly place** and there will always be outsiders who want to do harm to your firm.

The person in the firm who will be most interested in what is being done to defend against attacks on IT systems will be the **CFO**. When discussing vulnerability management with the CFO, the CIO needs to explain that at its heart it's really just the principals involved in **risk management** combined with **practical logic** and an understanding of **business value** for the firm.

How To Do Vulnerability Management

Although a CIO won't actually perform the process of Vulnerability Management, he /she is responsible for ensuring that the program is **set up correctly**. This means that the three key components of a Vulnerability Management program need to be put in place:

- **Data Collection Needs To Be Integrated**: Attacks on your IT systems rarely show up all at once. Instead, there is a sequence of minor events that occur as your defenses are probed looking for weaknesses. Having all of your data on system configurations, patch status, and access management policies in one place is a critical part of providing you with the ability to identify issues and respond proactively.

- **Prioritize Based On Business Value**: Look, we are all busy and have too little time and budget to begin with. If you understand the value of each IT system, then you can allocate resources appropriately. Not all events require a full blown response – low value systems can be monitored further. Defenses for such can be augmented on your schedule as opposed to on an emergency schedule.

- **Improve, Improve, Improve**: Vulnerability management is not something that can be done once and then forgotten about. The world is constantly changing and your program will need to be constantly being refined to adapt to new threats.

Final Thoughts

A CIO can do a great job of empowering the rest of the company to accomplish wonderful things; however, if the firm's IT systems are compromised then all of the good that he/she has done will be **forgotten in a flash**. A well- executed vulnerability management program provides a way to defend the firm against a cruel world. CIOs who follow the three steps that we've discussed will have **found a way** to apply IT to enable the rest of the company to grow quicker, move faster, and do more.

Chapter 4

Security Policies Are What CIOs Know Make Good Security Solutions

Chapter 4: Security Policies Are What CIOs Know Make Good Security Solutions

What does it take to do a really good job of securing your company's systems and data? Is it just a matter of picking and implementing the right software or hardware solution? Is there a consulting firm that you can pay millions to who will come in and take care of this problem once and for all? Bad news – the answer is **no**.

How Policies Make a Security Program Work

Securing a firm's systems and data is a daunting task. The first step to successfully doing this is to develop a risk management program that captures and describes all of the various internal and external risks that your firm is currently facing. Next comes the **prioritization of risks,** which allows you to determine which of these risks is most likely to affect your firm – **all risks are not created equal**.

Once you have prioritized the risks that your firm is facing, the CIO needs to step in and make sure that a program of **actionable policies** is created in order to secure your systems. All too often, this is the step that gets skipped and no matter how much technology you throw at the security problem, if you don't have a good set of polices you'll **never** be able to secure your systems.

Polices Secure Your Systems from Day-To-Day

What too many CIOs tend to forget is that the key to any company's security program is the **human element** and you manage this by having a clearly understood set of policies in place. Creating the policies is a first step, making sure that everyone knows about the policies and is living them are the next steps.

Kevin Mitnick is a reformed computer hacker who tours the country talking to businesses about the importance of securing their systems. I had an opportunity to hear him talk recently and it was amazing to hear how he **acquired** the information that he needed to break into company computer systems.

Kevin used a technique called "social engineering" in which he would basically call up someone and ask them for **sensitive system information**. No matter if the firms had a corporate security policy in effect, Kevin was basically able to get the people that he called to violate it. No, they weren't angry with their company, they were just trying too hard **to be helpful**. That's what can happen if you don't have security policies that are well known by everyone.

Final Thoughts

Doing a risk analysis and prioritizing the results is easy for IT professionals to do. However, creating policies that need to be followed by humans and then actually convincing their coworkers to follow the policies **can be a real challenge.**

A CIO can ensure that security policies will be successful by publicly stating his / her support for the policies and then **by following them**. Everyone will know if the CIO takes the polices seriously and by showing that you do, you will have **found a way** to apply IT to enable the rest of the company to grow quicker, move faster, and do more.

Chapter 5

Data Protection Secrets: CIOs Know That It Starts At the Endpoint

Chapter 5: Data Protection Secrets: CIOs Know That It Starts At the Endpoint

Just imagine this scenario: you've just been made CIO of your firm when all of a sudden one of your competitors suffers a massive data loss because of outside hackers. Your CEO storms into your brand-new office and demands to know what you are doing to secure your firm's data. **What would you say?**

The Old Way of Doing Things

Good CIOs realize that a firm's IT infrastructure can't just be thought of "those boxes". Instead, an IT infrastructure consists of **three layers** of devices: core servers and perhaps mainframes, a set of network connectivity devices such as routers and hubs, and then endpoints – the PCs and laptops that you and I use every day.

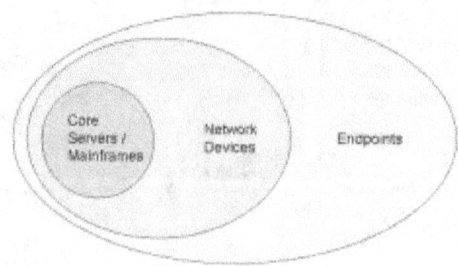

IT Networks Consist Of 3 Separate Levels of Equipment

Since there are **more endpoints** than any other type of equipment in most corporate networks, CIOs realize that this is where most of their company data loss efforts must be focused.

In the past, securing network endpoints often meant that all one had to do was to load up some **anti-virus software** on every laptop and you could check this off of your CIO to-do list. Sorry – that no longer works.

Welcome to The Real World

As we enter the brave new world of **policy management**, we are seeing a shift to policy-based enforcement being used to control company data that is being used on enterprise network endpoints.

Using policy-base management of endpoints allows **multiple areas** to be managed. These areas include:

- Configuration
- Patch
- Access
- Application
- Anti-virus

The Case for Using Policy-Based Management of Endpoints

Let's face it – we all have too much to do and too little time in which to get it all done. Establishing corporate IT polices allows **a set of rules** to be laid down that tells everyone what is and is not permitted. When you extend these polices to cover how you manage the endpoints of the company's network, then all of a sudden you've made your life that much easier.

Policies allow you to **prioritize the company information** that you want to protect. Once you identify this information, you'll then be able to realize just how much of it is being stored on the endpoints!

This new understanding then allows you to set up a **systems security** approach to making your PCs and laptops safe. By doing this you'll be able to ensure that your network endpoints are now secure places to house that valuable corporate data.

Final Thoughts

There's no way that any one person in an IT department can make sure that all of your PCs and laptops are secure all the time – even if you are the CIO. Yesterday's **piecemeal approach** of placing an anti-virus application on each PC and then considering the job done was a poor solution.

Using a **system's approach** and establishing company policies for how management of endpoints should be done sets up a much simpler way of ensuring that all endpoints are secure. CIOs that do this will have **found a way** to apply IT to enable the rest of the company to grow quicker, move faster, and do more.

Chapter 6

Application Whitelisting Only Works Sometimes – CIOs Need To Know the Facts

Chapter 6: Application Whitelisting Only Works Sometimes – CIOs Need To Know the Facts

It's a battle out there: hackers and organized crime groups vs. your company. Whereas you have to worry about keeping the company successful and lowering costs, all they have to worry about is finding ways to **break into your network**. Doesn't seem very fair, does it? There is some good news for CIOs: application whitelisting has arrived.

What is Whitelisting?

The problem with trying to protect your company's network is that the bad guys are always trying new and innovative things. In order to block them, you have to stay on top of what the latest attach vector is and install defenses against it throughout your network. This can be a real time waster – it's critical to do, but it contributes nothing to **the company's bottom line**.

Whitelisting applications takes a 180-degree different approach to securing your network. Instead of trying to identify and block all of the bad malware variants that are trying to get into your network, whitelisting focuses on identifying all of the applications that **SHOULD** be allowed to access your network.

This of course means that you need to block everything that is not whitelisted. The theory is that all that malware that shows up will find the door to your network **slammed shut** on them.

Whitelisting Is Not For Everyone

In some enterprise IT environments, whitelisting is the wrong way to go. In these environments, using application whitelisting can actually **drive up operational costs** so high that things quickly get out of hand. Ill-suited IT environments are those in which workers need to be constantly installing new and changed applications on the fly in order to complete their tasks.

Where Whitelisting Works Well

That being said, there are IT environments in which application whitelisting works very well. These environments tend to be **very static** with very few application changes. A great example of this is **call centers**.

Another example where whitelisting has worked well is in the retail sector where **cash register environments** are very static and only need to be updated every six months. Some companies have discovered that they have been able to do away with anti-virus protection (and the associated cost of maintaining it) on those machines.

Final Thoughts

The fight to secure the company's network from the forces that would do bad things to it is never-ending for CIOs. However, this is not what CIOs should be spending their time on – there is not a **bottom line benefit**.

Whitelisting of applications provides yet another way to secure the firm's network by taking **a novel approach to security** – don't worry about identifying the bad guys, just worry about identifying the good guys.

Whitelisting won't work for every environment, but in certain static IT environments **it can work wonders**. CIOs who can identify the right IT environments in which to use application whitelisting will have **found a way** to apply IT to enable the rest of the company to grow quicker, move faster, and do more.

Chapter 7

Halt Who Goes There? CIOs Need Good Identity Management

Chapter 7: Halt – Who Goes There? CIOs Need Good Identity Management

As though keeping all of those servers up, applications running, and end users happy seems like enough to make being CIO a full-time job, now CIOs also have to take on the role of data cop? The answer to this question is "yes", in all honesty, they really should already be doing it.

Most company's **most valuable asset**, after their employees, is their corporate data. CIOs need to find a way to make sure that they know who is accessing it and why.

Just What Is Identity Management?

Identity management is how an organization controls **access to its information** based on an individual's rights and responsibilities. It turns out that most IT shops have been doing a pretty poor job of this.

All too often most of us rely on our old friends **Mr. Username and Mr. Password**. How many dictionary based cracking events do we need to see in the movies in order to convince us that this is a very poor way to secure our data?

The right way to start to authenticate identities better is to use a **second-factor authentication system** such as biometrics, tokens, etc. Additionally, using single sign-on technologies can help you bring disparate systems together and save the end users from having to carry around lists of usernames/passwords.

What's The Best Way To Do Identity Management?

The first step to creating a workable identity management solution is to **establish some policies**. These policies need to lay out just who is allowed to access what information. Clearly, if you're not allowed to use some piece of information as a part of your job, then you shouldn't have access to it.

One of the biggest pitfalls that is found in IT departments today is the existence of multiple different "**silos**" of data that end up creating a confusing and mixed up environment for access control. Once again, implementing a single-signon solution can solve this problem.

Final Thoughts

Taking the time to design and implement a good identity management solution is very much like **buying insurance** for your IT department. You hope that you don't really need it, but you know that you probably do and it's the grown-up thing to do.

Taking the time to solve your identity management issues once and for all will allow a CIO to have **found a way** to apply IT to enable the rest of the company to grow quicker, move faster, and do more.

Chapter 8

The Insider Threat: What CIOs Need to Know

Chapter 8: The Insider Threat: What CIOs Need To Know

When you think about someone trying to make off with your company's private data, what comes to mind? Some wily Russian hacker who sneaks into your company's network through the backdoor? Perhaps you need to update your thinking. A recent report from Cisco revealed that the real threat is coming from **insiders**. What's a CIO to do?

Identifying the Threat

By now all CIOs realize that their corporate networks and data are under almost constant assault. However, most of the steps that CIOs have taken to secure their networks have been designed to defend themselves against the attacker **who comes from the outside**.

Information that was revealed in the Cisco report included that workers are sharing corporate information with outsiders for **a variety of reasons**. These include sharing data simply in order to get an outsider's opinion on something, to show off work that they've done to others, etc.

On top of the active taking of corporate data, Cisco's report revealed that some 66% of those who responded admitted to engaging in activities that would **allow someone else to access** corporate data (things like not logging off and then leaving their computers on at work overnight!)

Data Loss Prevention

If a CIO ever wants to get to sleep again, something has to be done to solve the data loss threat that insiders pose to the firm.

There is no magic bullet, but one approach to dealing with this problem is to deploy a **data loss prevention (DLP)** suite of tools.

In true "big brother" fashion, a DLP suite generally consists of a **network scanner** coupled with multiple tools that allow an IT department to collect information on what data is being used and by whom.

Before moving forward with implementing a DLP solution, CIOs need to take the time to **prepare** to use this new set of tools. The steps involved include:

- **Secure The Important Stuff**: before you go worrying about trying to secure how data is used throughout the enterprise, first identify the most important data and ensure that it is locked down.

- **Close Your (Network) Doors**: before you can worry about insiders doing you harm, you need to make sure that outsiders can't get in. This requires analyzing both your network ports and the protocols that the company's network is using to make sure that they are secure.

- **Create A Baseline**: in order to detect when the wrong things are being done, you need some way to detect them. Creating baselines such as point-in-time content signatures for sensitive data stores is a first step in doing this.

- **Start Inspecting Traffic**: the way that you can prevent information from going to internal sources that don't have a need to know is by installing automated network traffic inspectors. Setting parameters so that notifications of data breeches are flagged will do a great deal to prevent data loss by internal threats.

Final Thoughts

The value that a CIO brings to a firm is that he / she is able to harness IT resources in order to help the company succeed. As part of this task, the CIO is also responsible to make sure that sensitive **corporate data remains secure** from both external and internal threats.

CIOs that learn how to deploy DLP solutions in order to protect against the data loss threat from insiders will be better at finding ways to apply IT to enable the rest of the company to **grow quicker, move faster, and do more**.

Chapter 9

Poisonous Snakes, Sharp Knives and Angry Natives: How Much Risk Can You Handle?

Chapter 9: Poisonous Snakes, Sharp Knives, And Angry Natives: How Much Risk Can You Handle?

Ok CIO wannabe, we're right in the middle of a global financial crisis and your IT budget has gotten slashed so much it looks like Freddie Krueger has come back and had his way with it. What are you going to do about your spending on **security programs?** Cut 'em, hold the line, or spend more. Whoops – that was a trick question: all of the answers will get you in trouble.

What the Other Guys Are Doing

Before making any big spending decision, any self-respecting CIO will do what all leaders do – try to find out **what the other guys are doing** in the hopes that you can just copy them. Well, in this case you'll be getting mixed signals.

A survey done by Information Week magazine revealed that 19% of CIOs are **cutting their security spending**. On top of that, only 27% of the surveyed CIOs are planning on increasing their security budgets – that leaves roughly 50% doing the same old thing.

It's starting to look as though the final remaining sacred cow of IT budgets, spending on securing the enterprise's IT assets, has finally fallen under the budget trimming axe. This is an excellent opportunity to **learn how to be a better CIO**: cut too little and the company goes under, cut too much and the company may get sued when your defenses are breached.

What's Worse: Poisonous Snakes or Sharp Knives?

Here's another part of your CIO quiz: when your security budget comes under fire and you know that you're not going to be able to save the whole platoon, who do you pick to live and who do you let die? Tough call eh? That Information Week CIO survey revealed that most CIOs have decided that any security program that deals with **compliance** in some way, shape, or form needs to be saved.

In the end, CIOs are finally starting to realize that an effective corporate IT security policy consists of just **two things**:

- Managing Risk
- Protecting Data

Don't Forget About The Angry Natives - How CIOs Prioritize

If the job was easy, then anyone could be a CIO. The CIOs who get it, those who understand what effective IT security is really trying to do, know that the first thing that they have to do is to determine the company's overall **appetite for risk**. If the company has an appetite for a lot of risk, then the CIO can trim the IT security budget to the bone. Otherwise, cut with care!

Successful CIOs realize that the right way to go about setting up an IT security program is to start by realizing that **you can't protect everything** to the same level and so you need to identify what IT assets are the most valuable to the company. Once you know this, you need to take the next step and estimate the likelihood that those assets might be lost.

Only after you have both of these pieces of information can a CIO have the IT team start to **create security programs** and put systems of controls in place to protect what needs to be protected. Although compliance programs are on everyone's minds in these tough economic times, CIOs need to keep in mind that such programs are not always in line with security best practices.

Final Thoughts

If you want to have any hope of ever being a successful CIO, you've got to learn to be able to make the **tough calls** when it comes to funding corporate IT security programs. Although putting measures in place in order to make sure that the company remains complaint with regulations is good, it's not nearly enough.

Taking the time to properly value your corporate IT assets and identifying what kinds of risks this data faces is the critical first step that too many CIOs skip over. Take the time to do this correctly and you'll be **well positioned** to deal with poisonous snakes, sharp knives, and angry natives. Now if we could just find some way to deal with those pesky rampaging elephants...

Chapter 10

The Machines May Be Virtual, but the Security Problem Is Real

Chapter 10: The Machines May Be Virtual, but the Security Problem Is Real

When you become CIO, you already knew that **IT security** is going to be one of your biggest and least rewarding challenges. If you do a great job at it, then nobody will ever know and you'll get no credit for it. If you do a poor job, then everyone will know and you'll get all the blame. That just goes with the CIO job.

In the future, CIOs are going to have a whole new set of security issues that come along with the popularity of **virtual machines**. The rules for how best to secure these boxes that really aren't boxes have not been established yet. What can you do to make yourself ready to take on this new challenge?

Just What Is A Virtual Machine?

Before we dive in and start talking about security, let's make sure that we're all onboard when it comes to just exactly what a virtual machine is. Awhile back, some very smart folks (a lot of who happened to work at a company called Vmware) realized that most companies were deploying **one application per server** in their data centers: one for email, one for web hosting, etc.

It turns out that as servers got more powerful, this was incredibly ineffective – most of the server's processing power was not being used. The smart people created what they called a virtual machine (or VM) – software that sat on the server **between the actual server hardware and the operating system** that was running on the server. You can sort of think of it as a lower level operating system

Once this VM was in place, they discovered that they could run multiple operating systems (and then of course multiple applications on top of those operating systems) on each individual server. When they did this, **everything was isolated**, if one operating system crashed, it didn't interfere with the other operating systems / applications running on the same box.

As you can well imagine, this has turned out to be an incredibly popular way to **reduce the number of servers** that have to be deployed and maintained within a data center. However, it has also opened the door to some nasty security problems...

The Problem with Virtualization Security

Oh sure, you **THINK** that you know how to secure a data center – lock down all of the network ports going in and out, and then take steps to make sure that you know which staff are allowed to enter and leave. Uh oh, when your servers stop being real physical boxes and start to become virtual images, now you've going to have a whole new set of problems to deal with.

Cameron Sturdevant has been looking into just how we can go about securing the brave new future of virtual machines and he's uncovered **ten new issues** that you are going to have to be able to deal with:

Moving Too Fast: since virtual machines can be set up and put into operation much quicker than a real server can, you're going to have to set up some sort of review process in order to keep things under control.

Redefine Your Boundaries: it used to be simple to be able to keep the important things inside the data center and the threats outside when everything needed a physical box. Now that things are going virtual, these boundaries are getting more murky and you will have to spend the time to redraw them.

Killed By Quantity: since it's so easy to set up a new virtual machine, you're going to be facing an explosion of them. This means that you're going to have to establish a policy to determine when a new virtual machine needs to be deployed and when it needs to be turned off.

Moving Day Is Every Day: since virtual machines can easily move from box to box, you're going to have to lay down the law in order to make sure that the new server has the appropriate security policies in place in order to support the applications that will be running on it.

Not the Same As The Old Boss: both the tools and the policies that used to work in the world of "real" servers won't necessarily work in the new world of virtual servers. You're going to have to find / make new ones.

Virtual Tools: in order to police your virtual machines, you are going to want your security tools to run on virtual machines also – makes sense, doesn't it?

Cutting Costs: how many CPU cycles your virtual security tools take up will be a huge deal very quickly. The rule of thumb is for them to take less than 2-3% of the CPU's cycles.

Policy Update Time: not only will you need fancy new tools, but you are also going to need to update your staff on just how one goes about securing virtual boxes. Can you say special training?

Where to Focus?: The experts suggest that you spend your time securing both the virtual machine and its applications and don't worry so much about the underlying virtual machines. The thinking is that virtual machines are by design isolated from everything else so they are more secure.

Get Some Relief: look for virtual machine management tools that will allow your staff to automate the processes of configuring and deploying virtual machines as much as possible in order to minimize security slipups.

Final Thoughts

Like it or not, when you become CIO you're going to be living in a virtual world. All of the clever security tools and policies that we've created in an attempt to secure the world of physical servers that we now live in are **not going to work** in the future.

Your challenge will be to find ways to secure the virtual data center while at the same time keeping your IT staff's workload at a manageable level. The good news is that **this can be done**, the bad news is that you're going to be in uncharted territory. Good luck future CIO...!

Chapter 11

Why CIOs May Be the Company's Biggest Security Risk

Chapter 11: Why CIOs May Be The Company's Biggest Security Risk

The world is **a very dangerous place**. Your IT department has lots and lots of data on its computers that bad people would like to get their hands on. Thank goodness your company has taken care to secure every way that there is for outsiders to get into your company's network. Oh, wait a minute. Maybe there's one way that hasn't been secured – you!

What We Are Doing Wrong

Over the last 30 years or so, corporations have spent untold billions of dollars to create **secure corporate networks**. The definition of information technology tells us that we need to use firewalls to keep the bad guys out and strict corporate policies to restrict just exactly what can be connected to the corporate network.

That's all fine and good until you, the CIO, come along. For a couple of very important reasons **you may be your company's single greatest security threat**. The first of these reasons is simply because you know too much. In your head is a lot of information that both hackers and your company's IT sector competition would love to get their hands on.

This means that every action that you take online runs the risk of **exposing confidential company information to the outside world**. This could be as simple as when you update your LinkedIn profile with what you are currently working on to when you use your personal Gmail account while you are at work.

The second way that you may be your company's biggest security threat is by **your love of all that is new and shiny**. CIOs are notorious for being the first kids on the block to go out and buy the latest tech gadget no matter if it's the latest iPhone or iPad. Once you have this fantastic new device and you start to use it all the time, you'll of course bring it into work. When you do this, you run all sorts of risks.

Hanging a Sign Out

If you were a bad guy and you wanted to break into your company's corporate network, how would you go about doing it? Considering that companies have had enough time to secure their corporate networks from people breaking in from the outside, you'd probably do the next best thing: **try to break in from the inside**.

You'd go about doing this by finding out who worked for the company. Then you'd engage in a little of what's called **"spear phishing"**. This is when you send someone who works for the company an email that looks like it is coming from somebody else inside the company asking for usernames, passwords, nuclear launch codes, etc.

We've all been trained to not respond to spam emails that we get all the time. However, these spear phishing ones are a lot harder to detect because **they look like they are legit**. We can become a phishing target by sharing a lot of personal information on the web. LinkedIn is prime hunting ground for those would like to do us harm – there is a lot of key information shared out there.

Doing It Ourselves

Another way that we can cause great harm to the company is when we bring our newest and shiniest electronic gadget with us to work. As the Iranians found out with their centrifuge machines, a computer from home can contain all sorts of **nasty viruses and bad things**.

The company has polices about what can be connected to the corporate network and what public web sites we are allowed to use while at work. As CIO you may believe that **these rules don't apply to you**; however, that's where you'd be wrong. Yes, the rules might be an inconvenience sometimes, but they were created for a reason.

Couple all of the standard threats and then add in today's popular **social media sites** and you have a real problem on your hands. The fact that hackers can reach out to you via numerous social media sites means that they are just that much closer to getting into your corporate network.

What We Need To Be Doing

So clearly it's a big scary world out there and **we are not immune** from taking steps to be part of the solution, not the problem. What should we be doing?

First off, just make it a personal rule that you'll never email any **confidential information** such as user names or passwords to anyone no matter if you think that they work for the company or not. If somebody needs that information, have them come to your office and pick it up.

Next, make it a policy to **never open any attachments** that have been added to an email that you've received. This is how the bad guys get you to run code that opens up doors into your corporate network for them. Make it a habit to not open any attachments until you get into a meeting or a call where the person who you think sent it to you can confirm that they really did.

What All of This Means For You

So now that we understand that the single greatest threat to the safety of our company's digital assets may be us, **what does all of this mean?** It's actually pretty straightforward. We need to become more responsible in how we behave because of importance of information technology to our company.

We need to always be aware of the fact that there are people out there who are always looking for a way to **break into our company's computers**. Due to our special position in the company, if we're not careful then our actions may open a door for them to gain access to the company's network.

I like the newest flashy device just as much as you do. However, when it comes to keeping the company's network safe, it appears as though we need to **separate our personal life (and devices) from those that we use at work**. Don't worry – eventually all good things will find their way into our office the right way!

Chapter 12

Why CIOs Can't Believe
All That They Read
About Security Breeches

Chapter 12: Why CIOs Can't Believe All That They Read About Security Breeches

If a CIO picks up the paper, it seems like hackers are everywhere and getting into every IT department. Dare I say **these modern day cyber pirates seem almost unstoppable?** If it turns out that there is no way to keep hackers from breaking into your company's IT systems, then should a CIO really spend a lot of time and money trying to keep them out?

The Myth of the Super Hacker

If you spend any time reading the newspapers, it can be easy to feel that **every company out there is under assault**. Teams of skilled hackers who go by names such as LulzSec and Anonymous seem to be in the news every other day as they take down or deface various high profile web sites. This type of assault has almost become part of the definition of information technology.

No matter what safeguards these firms seem to have had in place, still the hackers seem to be able to **slip by them** and have their way with the company's IT systems. What's a CIO to do?

The first thing that you need to do is realize that **you can't lump all hackers together**. Yes, there are some very skillful hackers out there who have the ability to cause a great deal of grief for any company in the IT sector that they decide to target. However, the good news is that the majority of hackers are not so skillful.

When you are reading the newspaper, you need to take a close look at **what actually occurred** as a result of a hacking exploit. Did a talented hacker break in and steal valuable customer data? Or, did the company just suffer a distributed denial of service attack (DDOS) – a much less skillful form of digital vandalism?

Not all hackers are created the same, and CIOs need to take steps to protect their company from the majority of hackers who are **simply looking for an unguarded door** that will allow them to break into your digital warehouse of customer data.

What CIOs Need To Do To Defend the Company

All of this discussion leads us back to the basic question: **what should a CIO do?** The very first thing that a CIO needs to do is to not give up hope. Don't just assume that all criminal hackers are gods. The reality is that most are not. This means that you can't afford to let your guard down because in most cases the basic steps that you take to secure the company will be good enough to keep most of the bad guys out.

This won't keep the really bad, really skillful guys out. This is when your so-called **second layer of defense** needs to come into play. As a CIO you are going to have to assume that a skilled hacker who really wants to break into your company's IT systems is going to be able to climb over the wall of defenses that you've put into place.

The question then comes down to what they'll find once they are in. If you make it easy for them, like T.J. Maxx did when 45 million of their customer records were exposed to hackers, then they'll be able to run wild. However, **this doesn't have to be the case**.

If you anticipate this type of event happening and set up safeguards, you can **minimize the amount of damage that a skillful hacker can cause**. One of the simplest steps that you can take is to encrypt all customer data that flows between your internal systems.

What a step like this means is that even if a hacker gets inside of your company's IT systems, he or she **won't be able to easily get their hands on your valuable customer data**. Additionally, rogue employees, a much greater threat than skilled hackers, will also be unable to walk off with your company's crown jewels.

It's the responsibility of the CIO to **consider likely scenarios like this**. Once you've identified something that could happen, you are then obligated to take all of the necessary steps that will be needed in order to protect the company against lawsuits, fines, investigations, and, of course, post-event cleanup activities.

What All Of This Means For You

Welcome to the real world CIO – stuff happens here. Specifically, there are always going to be hackers out there who are looking for companies to break into. **Your company could be next on their list**.

If you take a look at all of the stories that are being reported in the press lately, it sure seems as though the hackers who are operating these days seem to be able to effortlessly slip into and out of any company that they choose. **Nobody seems to be safe**.

However, if you take a closer look, things become a bit clearer. Specifically, what you'll discover is that there are actually **two types of hacking going on**: the simple distributed denial of service attacks and the more sophisticated break-ins. You may not be able to protect the company against an attack by skillful, educated hackers. However, you can take steps such as encrypting your data so that even if they do get in, the amount of damage that they can cause will be minimized.

CIOs can't give up. The importance of information technology to your company is too great. Yes, the bad guys are going to win some of the battles. However, that doesn't mean that the war is over. Instead, CIOs need to **take steps** to make sure that most hackers can't get in and the ones that do can't do much once they do get in. Make the effort now and you and your company will be safe later on.

It's from the forge of failure that the steel of success is formed.

Hard Work Does Not Guarantee Success, But Success Does Not Happen Without Hard Work.

- Dr. Jim Anderson

Create IT Departments That Are Productive And A Valuable Asset To The Rest Of The Company !

Dr. Jim Anderson is available to provide training and coaching on the topics that are the most important to people who have to manage IT departments: how can I build a productive IT department (and keep it together) while at the same time providing the rest of the company with the IT services that they need?

Dr. Anderson believes that in order to both learn and remember what he says, speakers need to laugh. Each one of his speeches is full of fun and humor so that what he says "sticks" with everyone.

Dr. Anderson's CIO SkillsTraining Includes:

4. How to identify and attract the right type of IT workers to your IT department.
5. How to build relationships with the company's senior management in order to get the support that you need?
6. How to stay on top of changing technology and security issues so that you never get surprised?

Dr. Jim Anderson works with over 100 customers per year. To invite Dr. Anderson to work with you, contact him at:

Phone: 813-418-6970 or
Email: jim@BlueElephantConsulting.com

Blue
Elephant
Consulting

Speaking.   Negotiating.   Managing.   Marketing.

Photo Credits:

Cover - By: FutUndBeidl
https://www.flickr.com/photos/61423903@N06/

Chapter 1 - By: Dr. Jim Anderson

Chapter 2 – By: StockMonkeys.com
www.StockMonkeys.com

Chapter 3 - By: Mike Licht
www.NotionsCapital.com

Chapter 4 – By: Elhombredenegro
https://www.flickr.com/photos/77519207@N02/

Chapter 5 - By: European Parliament
https://www.flickr.com/photos/european_parliament/

Chapter 6 - By: Bust it Away Photography
http://bustitawayphotography.com/

Chapter 7 - By: JF Sebastian
https://www.flickr.com/photos/jf-sebastian/

Chapter 8 - By: Nikita Borisov
https://www.flickr.com/photos/nikitab/

Chapter 9 - By: Kim Seng
https://www.flickr.com/photos/captainkimo/7555337066/

Chapter 10 - By: Sman5612
https://www.flickr.com/photos/25975072@N07/5466420409/
www.openclipart.org

Chapter 11 - By: Eisgrafin
https://www.flickr.com/photos/37116665@N04/

Chapter 12 - By: david white design
https://www.flickr.com/photos/davidandseb/

Other Books By The Author

Product Management

- How Product Managers Can Grow Their Career: How Product Managers Can Find And Succeed In The Right Job

- Product Management Secrets: Techniques For Product Managers To Boost Product Sales And Increase Customer Satisfaction

- Product Development Lessons For Product Managers: How Product Managers Can Create Successful Products

- Customer Lessons For Product Managers: Techniques For Product Managers To Better Understand What Their Customers Really Want

- Product Failure Lessons For Product Managers: Examples Of Products That Have Failed For Product Managers To Learn From

- Communication Skills For Product Managers: The Communication Skills That Product Managers Need

To Know How To Use In Order To Have A Successful Product

- How To Have A Successful Product Manager Career: The Things That You Need To Be Doing TODAY In Order To Have A Successful Product Manager Career

- Product Manager Product Success: How to keep your product on track and make it become a success

Public Speaking

- How To Become A Better Speaker By Changing How You Speak: Change techniques that will transform a speech into a memorable event

- How To Give A Great Presentation: Presentation techniques that will transform a speech into a memorable event

- How To Rehearse In Order To Give The Perfect Speech: How to effectively rehearse your next speech to that your message be remembered forever!

- Secrets To Creating The Perfect Speech: How to create a speech that will make your message be remembered forever!

- Secrets To Organizing The Perfect Speech: How to organize the best speech of your life!

- Secrets To Planning The Perfect Speech: How to plan to give the best speech of your life

- How To Show What You Mean During A Presentation: How to use visual techniques to transform a speech into a memorable event

CIO Skills

- What CIOs Need To Know About Working With Partners: Techniques For CIOs To Use In Order To Be Able To Successfully Work With Partners

- Critical CIO Management Skills: Decision Making Skills That Every CIO Needs To Have In Order To Be Able To Make The Right Choices

- How CIOs Can Make Innovation Happen: Tips And Techniques For CIOs To Use In Order To Make Innovation Happen In Their IT Department

- CIO Communication Skills Secrets: Tips And Techniques For CIOs To Use In Order To Become

Better Communicators

- Managing Your CIO Career: Steps That CIOs Have To Take In Order To Have A Long And Successful Career

- CIO Business Skills: How CIOs can work effectively with the rest of the company!

IT Manager Skills

- How IT Managers Can Make Innovation Happen: Tips And Techniques For IT Managers To Use In Order To Make Innovation Happen In Their Teams

- Staffing Skills IT Managers Must Have: Tips And Techniques That IT Managers Can Use In Order To Correctly Staff Their Teams

- Secrets Of Effective Leadership For IT Managers: Tips And Techniques That IT Managers Can Use In Order To Develop Leadership Skills

- IT Manager Career Secrets: Tips And Techniques That IT Managers Can Use In Order To Have A Successful Career

- IT Manager Budgeting Skills: How IT Managers Can Request, Manage, Use, And Track Their Funding

Negotiating

- Learn How To Signal In Your Next Negotiation: How To Develop The Skill Of Effective Signaling In A Negotiation In Order To Get The Best Possible Outcome

- Learn The Skill Of Exploring In A Negotiation: How To Develop The Skill Of Exploring What Is Possible In A Negotiation In Order To Reach The Best Possible Deal

- Learn How To Argue In Your Next Negotiation: How To Develop The Skill Of Effective Arguing In A Negotiation In Order To Get The Best Possible Outcome

- How To Open Your Next Negotiation: How To Start A Negotiation In Order To Get The Best Possible Outcome

- Preparing For Your Next Negotiation: What You Need To Do BEFORE A Negotiation Starts In Order To Get The Best Possible Deal

Miscellaneous

- The Internet-Enabled Successful School District Superintendent: How To Use The Internet To Boost Parental Involvement In Your Schools

- Power Distribution Unit (PDU) Secrets: What Everyone Who Works In A Data Center Needs To Know!

- Making The Jump: How To Land Your Dream Job When You Get Out Of College!

Tips And Techniques For CIOs To Use In Order To Secure Both Their IT Department And Their Company

This book has been written with one goal in mind – to show you how you can secure both your IT department and your company. It's not easy being a CIO so we're going to show you the strategies and techniques that you can use to keep the bad guys out of your IT department!

Let's Make Your CIO Career A Success!

What You'll Find Inside:

- **VULNERABILITY MANAGEMENT: THE CIO'S OTHER JOB**

- **KEVIN MITNICK SPEAKS ABOUT IT SECURITY**

- **DATA PROTECTION SECRETS: CIOS KNOW THAT IT STARTS AT THE ENDPOINT**

- **THE INSIDER THREAT: WHAT CIOS NEED TO KNOW**

Dr. Jim Anderson brings his 25 years of real-world experience to this book. He's been a senior IT executive at some of the world's largest firms. He's going to show you what you need to do (and not do!) in order to make your CIO career a success!

www.ingramcontent.com/pod-product-compliance
Lightning Source LLC
Chambersburg PA
CBHW071306170526
45165CB00003B/1440